The Wave

Inspiration for

Navigating Life's Changes & Challenges

The Wave

⤺ Inspiration for ⤻
Navigating Life's Changes & Challenges

Jane Seymour

WEST 26TH STREET PRESS
NEW YORK

The Wave: Inspiration for Navigating Life's Changes and Challenges
by Jane Seymour

Copyright © 2014 by Jane Seymour

ISBN 13: 978-1-63064-000-2

Printed in the United States of America

Edited by: Heather Maclean
Design by: Goshia Podlaska, M'Gosh Design

West 26th Street Press
21 West 26th Street
New York, NY 10010

Distributed to the trade by Ingram Publisher Services. For special sales,
please contact Spring House Press at info@springhousepress.com.

Dedication

For my family and friends

You lift me up when the waves get overwhelming,

share my joy when I'm riding the crest of the wave,

and all the time swim steadfastly alongside me.

I am blessed to share my life's journey with you.

Contents

Sea Change

I created this book to inspire those who, like myself, like all of us, are facing or have faced challenges or changes in their lives.

The cycle of life is so evident in the cyclical motion of the wave. It flows, it crests, it crashes, it lets go, it takes experience with it as it joins new water and connects with all its wisdom to become a new wave.

By opening our hearts and visualizing the "cycle of a wave," we may see that all experience, both good and bad, is simply a part of the "cycle of life." It isn't always a pleasant process, but if we're open to it, the results can be more wonderful than we ever imagined.

—Jane Seymour

Full fathom five thy father lies;
Of his bones are coral made;
Those are pearls that were his eyes:

Nothing of him that doth fade,
But doth suffer a sea-change
Into something rich and strange.

—*William Shakespeare,* The Tempest

Jane Seymour

Family Waves

You Are Not Alone

When a crisis happens in our lives, it's so easy to feel alone. We must remember that like drops in the ocean, we are all connected. We are all part of something larger than ourselves. We are all family. We aren't always up or down at the same time, but we are on the same journey together. By opening our hearts to one another, we can help each other appreciate both the dips and the swells of life.

—Jane Seymour

Launch Yourself on Every Wave

You must live in the present, launch yourself on every wave, find your eternity in each moment. Fools stand on their island of opportunities and look toward another land. There is no other land, there is no other life but this.

—Henry David Thoreau

Infinite Opportunities

Let the wave of life wash over us and carry us a little farther up the shore. The breaking of a wave is only the beginning!

—*Cheri Ingle*

We Must Learn to Sail

We must free ourselves of the hope

that the sea will ever rest.

We must learn to sail in high winds.

—Aristotle Onassis

Don't Give Up the Ship

My husband and I met in the Navy. I'm now a reservist raising our kids, but he's been active for fourteen years. He was recently deployed to Afghanistan. He had been deployed before, but this deployment seemed like no other. I constantly worried about his safety and well-being. Everything seemed to go wrong when he was gone. When it rains, it pours. There were so many days that I just wanted to give up. But we have a saying in the Navy—"Don't give up the ship!" It's something I take to heart. If you don't give up, you can stay afloat long enough for the winds to change and things to get better.

—Deanna

Jane Seymo

Home on the Rolling Deep

A life on the ocean wave,

A home on the rolling deep,

Where the scattered waters rave,

And the winds their revels keep!

Like an eagle caged, I pine

On this dull, unchanging shore:

Oh! give me the flashing brine,

The spray and the tempest's roar!

—*Epes Sargent*

Footsteps in the Sea

God moves in a mysterious way,

His wonders to perform.

He plants his footsteps in the sea,

And rides upon the storm.

—William Cowper

The Captain of My Soul

I am the master of my fate:
I am the captain of my soul.

—William Ernest Henley

Shared Strength

My family has always meant everything to me. After caring for my ill son and husband for many years and then losing them both to cancer, I naively thought things could only get better. How wrong I was! My younger daughter was then diagnosed with cancer, too. How do you go on when your world is torn apart again? You do because it's the only way to survive. You do because if you don't swim, you'll sink. You keep moving forward, but you can't do it alone. You need relatives, neighbors, friends, and sometimes even perfect strangers to give you strength.

—Mari

There Is a Tide

There is a tide in the affairs of men,

Which, taken at the flood, leads on to fortune;

Omitted, all the voyage of their life

Is bound in shallows and in miseries.

On such a full sea are we now afloat,

And we must take the current when it serves,

Or lose our ventures.

—*William Shakespeare*, Julius Caesar

On the Crest

...People feel that they must perpetually
be on the crest of the wave, not realising
that it is against all the rules of life.
You can't be on top all the time;
it isn't natural.

—Olivia De Havilland

The Flow of Life

This past year has been a very difficult year at best. My mom suffered from a kidney disease and ended up in hospice. Dad bought Mom one of your beautiful necklaces with waves made of open hearts. It helped her to feel like she was in control of her destiny, riding on top of the waves, and to know that she was beautiful even in the midst of illness. After Mom passed away, my dad gave me the necklace. I wear it almost every day as a reminder to keep my heart open and to go with the flow of life.

—*Gail*

Relationship Waves

Waves of Change

We are born and go through life as if part of a body of water that crests when we find joy or success, and sometimes crashes. As the crash occurs, many of us stop in our tracks and say, "Why me? Why now?"

Instead of signaling destruction, however, the crash can simply signal change. Just as a wave lets go of the water it doesn't need and regroups with new water, forming a new wave, when we let go of the broken and gone—the relationship, the job, the profession, the picture of perfection—we are open to new love, new life, and new possibilities.

—Jane Seymour

We Cannot Exist Alone

Just as the wave cannot exist for itself,

but is ever a part of the heaving surface of the ocean,

so must I never live my life for itself,

but always in the experience which is going on around me.

—Albert Schweitzer

Never Stay Broken

My husband of thirteen years left me with two young children. They cried for hours the day he left. I read Jane's words a long time ago and have kept them in my heart. I kept my heart open so that one day I would fall in love again. Six years after he left, I am marrying a wonderful man I met a few years back. The front of my wedding invitation states, "If your heart is open, it can never stay broken."

—Maria

cheri

A Great Tide of Love and Prayer

Out of the depths of my happy heart

wells a great tide of love and prayer for

this priceless treasure that is confided

to my life-long keeping.

You cannot see its intangible waves

as they flow toward you, darling,

but in these lines you will hear,

as it were, the distant beating of its surf.

—*Mark Twain, in a letter to his future wife, Olivia*

Stay the Course

No one would have crossed

the ocean if he could have gotten off

the ship in the storm.

—Charles Kettering

Hold the Helm

Anyone can hold the helm
when the sea is calm.

—*Publilius Syrus*

Cross the Sea

You can't cross the sea
merely by standing
and staring at the water.

—*Rabindranath Tagore*

Comfort One Another

When my sixteen-year-old son who lived with me all of his life decided to go live with his dad, I was devastated. I cried, and planned a pity party for myself until I heard that my neighbor's husband had died. I knew I had to put my sorrow aside for their family. Through tears, I baked apple dumplings, and then carried them across the street. I was greeted warmly at the door, visited with the family, and left with such an uplifting feeling. I thought, "If my neighbor can do this, I can survive my own problem, which seems so small compared to hers." We all have problems at various times in our lives, but by comforting and helping each other through the storms of life, we are able to make it through.

—Shelley

A Moving Sea

But let there be spaces in your togetherness and

let the winds of the heavens dance between you.

Love one another but make not a bond of love:

Let it rather be a moving sea between

the shores of your souls.

—Khalil Gibran

Jane Seymour

My Love, My Anchor

Six years ago, I lost my husband, my daughter's daddy, to cancer. Watching him suffer was the hardest thing we ever had to go through. He was the love of my life, my soul mate. When I lost him, I thought all was lost, including love. I felt adrift, like nothing would ever anchor me in happiness again. But I kept my heart open for the sake of my daughter. I'm so happy I did or I wouldn't have met Bill, my now-husband. Closing your heart, especially when times are tough, means you could be closing yourself off to exactly what you need to heal you again.

—Kim

The Cure

The cure for anything is salt water: sweat, tears, or the sea.

—*Isak Dinesen*

Jane Seymour

Friendship Waves

Constant Motion

Like the wave, life gives us the gift of

constant opportunities to grow and change.

Life is like a wave—

continuously building, cresting, and releasing . . .

always allowing for learning, connecting, and revival.

—Jane Seymour

Humanity Is an Ocean

You must not lose faith
in humanity. Humanity is
an ocean; if a few drops of
the ocean are dirty, the ocean
does not become dirty.

—*Gandhi*

Be Free, Be Divine

I am you; you are me.

You are the waves; I am the ocean.

Know this and be free, be divine.

—Sri Sathya Sai Baba

Open to Other Possibilities

Just as the ocean can turn a grain of sand into a pearl, God can use the bad things that happen to us in our lives for good later on. When I tried to have a second child, I became pregnant twice, but lost both babies. I was thirty-six, and didn't want to continue the pain of losing, so I had my tubes tied. As a career teacher, I'm always assigned a beginning teacher to mentor. My twenty-two-year-old first-year teacher had a childhood of disappointment because her mother chose an affair over her, and gave her to her dad to raise. I "adopted" her, and she became a member of our family. On the day she was married, I was honored to stay by her side until she was walked down the aisle. We had both suffered loss, but by leaving our hearts open to other possibilities that God had in store for us, I got the second child I had wanted, and she got the mother she had been without.

—Elizabeth

Rescued by Open Hearts

In November, I lost my husband of nineteen years unexpectedly. He was only fifty-five years old, and I had never thought that he would be taken from me so young. I was sad, depressed, and slowly killing myself through obesity. Fortunately, a couple of dear friends saw that I was drowning in my misery, and they loved me out of it. I started taking care of myself, eating healthy, and lost over two hundred pounds. I wanted to live to see my grandson grow up. Without the open hearts of my friends, I would not have survived.

—Laurie

Feel the Waves

There's no secret to balance. You just have to feel the waves.

—Frank Herbert

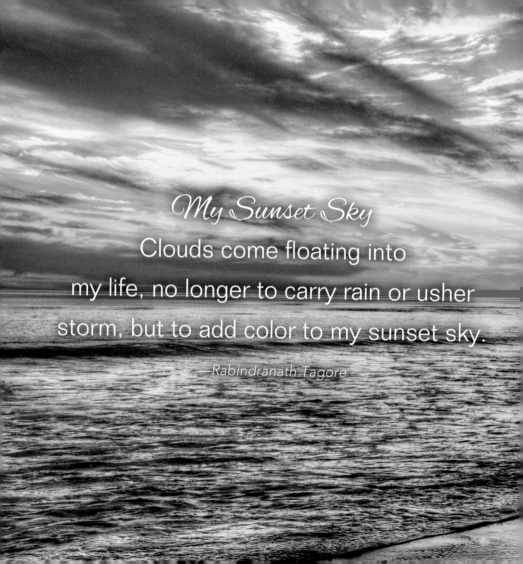

My Sunset Sky

Clouds come floating into
my life, no longer to carry rain or usher
storm, but to add color to my sunset sky.

-Rabindranath Tagore

By the Deep Sea

There is a pleasure in the pathless woods,

There is a rapture on the lonely shore,

There is society where none intrudes,

By the deep sea, and music in its roar;

I love not Man the less, but Nature more.

—Lord Byron

The Simplest Act Can Change the World

Growing up in a cold and distant family, I have struggled my entire life with letting people into my life and my heart. I wake up each morning telling myself to do one small act of kindness for another person. I have seen how even the simplest act can change someone's day. If all I can give that day is a smile, that is enough. When we are feeling at our worst, nothing can make us feel better than trying to make someone else feel better.

—Sue

Faith Waves

Jane Seymour

Constantly Moving and Changing

Just like the ocean, life is constantly moving and changing. The way we can handle this and move forward is to open our hearts to others who share similar tales. We connect to new relationships and possibilities. The change then becomes a gift.

—Jane Seymour

A Little Drop of Water

Everyone has faith in God though everyone does not know it. For everyone has faith in himself and that multiplied to the nth degree is God. The sum total of all that lives is God. We may not be God, but we are of God, even as a little drop of water is of the ocean.

—Gandhi

Who Stilled the Roaring of the Seas

Who formed the mountains by your power,

having armed yourself with strength,

who stilled the roaring of the seas,

the roaring of their waves,

and the turmoil of the nations.

The whole earth is filled with awe at your wonders;

where morning dawns, where evening fades,

you call forth songs of joy.

—*Psalm 65: 6–8*

Jane Seymour

Carried Through the Waves

My life has been a series of overwhelming changes. At thirty years old, I was the mom of two small children, married to my high school sweetheart, and living the life of my dreams. And then I was diagnosed with breast cancer. After surgery and grueling chemotherapy, I was cancer-free and thought I was done. But I wasn't. A year later, the cancer was back, and it had spread. I underwent more chemotherapy, radiation, and surgery. I lost all my hair and all of my energy, my breasts, my ovaries, and was thrown into menopause overnight. But I never lost faith.

Through it all, I stayed positive. Whenever anyone asks me how, I always give the same answer: God. God carried me through the waves of my life. He carried me when I didn't have the strength to swim or even to float. I knew no matter what happened that God was going to see me through it because He was more powerful than cancer. You have to have faith!

—Helen

The Deep Surrounded Me

I called out to the Lord, out of my distress,
and he answered me;
out of the belly of Sheol I cried,
and you heard my voice.
For you cast me into the deep,
into the heart of the seas,
and the flood surrounded me;
all your waves and your billows
passed over me . . .
The waters closed in over me to take my life;
the deep surrounded me;
weeds were wrapped about my head
at the roots of the mountains.
I went down to the land
whose bars closed upon me forever;
yet you brought up my life from the pit,
O Lord my God.

—Jonah 2: 2–6

All Waters Lead

As different streams having different sources all mingle their waters in the sea, so different tendencies, various though they appear, crooked or straight, all lead to God.

—*Swami Vivekananda*

Storm Waltzing

Waves come crashing around tomorrow with a temperament for uncertainty. Hardened hearts sit idle in the storm with their colorful umbrellas poised for the dancing waters. Nothing can come between the rock and the polishing waters of life. In its course, nature twists and turns like a mother giving birth. The rise and the fall of nature move us into God's ballroom or to sit deliriously on the shore and breathe under the guise of man's parasol of ineptitude. Multitudes of trials drift through the fog of humanity. The blinking lighthouses and the glimmering gulls frame existence as life dances with the storms or idly peer and jeer from a shore of manmade umbrellas. A sea of man's canopies cannot calm the storms; we are called to waltz into the awakening of each other's destiny. Waves come crashing around tomorrow with a temperament for uncertainty. In the shelter of the storms we move and have our being in God.

—Kathy Paysen

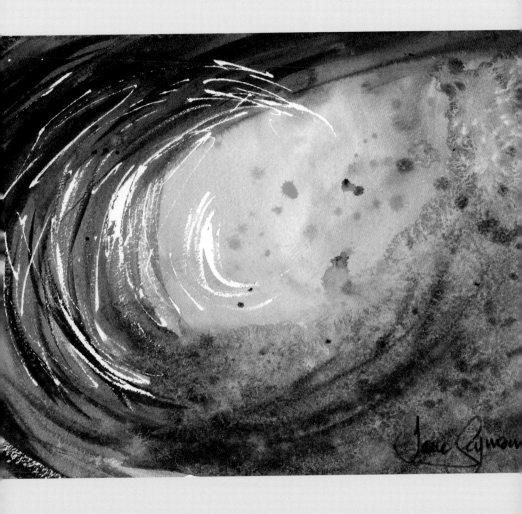

Surfacing from the Deep

I was in a very abusive relationship for a few years. It took everything I had mentally, but I got out. I had two little girls and struggled to raise them alone. Some days I felt like I was apart from the whole world, alone at the bottom of the ocean, but I knew deep down that I was meant for better. The following year, I found it. I found my soul mate: a guy who loved me and loved my two little girls like they were his own. We were so happy for five years, until one night when he was killed by a drunk driver. My whole world capsized in an instant. Once again I felt myself being dragged into the deep, but I knew he wouldn't want that for me. So, instead, I focused all my energy on doing things to keep him close to my heart and his memory alive. Each Christmas, I use the money I would have spent on his gift for an angel tree to help others without. I live each day showing those I love how much I appreciate them. It is because of my past heartbreaks that I have learned how precious a gift life is. You have to make the most of it, and truly can only do that with an open heart.

—Michelle

We Are in the Same Boat

The sea, the great unifier,
is man's only hope. Now, as never before,
the old phrase has a literal meaning:
we are all in the same boat.

—Jacques Yves Cousteau

Jane Seym

Health Waves

Life Rolls On

Just before he was about to turn pro, one of my good friends, surfer Jesse Billauer, was surfing at Zuma Beach when he hit a shallow sandbar and fractured his neck. His injuries resulted in quadriplegia. He lost the ability to walk, and had limited mobility of his arms and legs. But he did not lose his ability to hope. As soon as he left the hospital, he swore to do two things: surf again and help others follow their passions.

He did just that, founding the charity Life Rolls On (liferollson.org) and creating adaptive surfing, skating, and snowboarding programs that allow young people affected by spinal cord injuries to participate in action sports. Jesse's story reminds us all that anything is possible no matter what your situation, diagnosis, or prognosis. There is always room in an open heart for hope and love.

—Jane Seymour

Go Out in the Ocean

Either you decide to stay
in the shallow end of the pool
or you go out in the ocean.

—Christopher Reeve

The Secret of the Sea

My soul is full of longing

For the secret of the sea,

And the heart of the great ocean

Sends a thrilling pulse through me.

—Henry Wadsworth Longfellow

Rolling with the Change

I used to be a closed-minded, angry, unpleasant person. That all changed the day I found out I had a brain tumor. In response to that life-changing news, I changed my life forever.

I instantly changed the way I thought, acted, and loved. The tumor was removed, and I have lasting effects from the surgery, but I would not trade my diagnosis for anything. I learned how to let things roll off my shoulders as easily as water. I will not be weighed down! I can honestly say I am happier than I have ever been.

—Dawn

Undaunted

The fishermen know that the sea is dangerous and the storm terrible, but they have never found these dangers sufficient reason for remaining ashore.

—Vincent Van Gogh

Our Memories of the Ocean

Our memories of the ocean
will linger on, long after our
footprints in the sand are gone.

—Anonymous

Jane Seymour

A Swift-Moving Current

I am standing neck-deep in a swift-moving current; the world is standing fast all around me, secure in their place and unconcerned by the torrent passing by. Yet I am holding on by the slightest of branches; my anchor, my rock, taken from me.

—Drew Genneken

When Drew Genneken lost his fourteen-year-old son to leukemia because they couldn't find a bone marrow transplant match, he turned his grief into action. To honor his son's dying wish that no other child suffer as he did, Drew and his wife vowed to "play it forward." They founded the Tyler Genneken Foundation and host football tournaments to raise awareness and funds for the Be The Match Foundation, a nonprofit that matches bone marrow donors with potential recipients. Thanks to their efforts, several matches have already been made and precious lives saved.

Weathering the Storm

When I was diagnosed with breast cancer, I could have easily wallowed in my illness and let it suck me down under the waves of despair. But I didn't. I kept a positive attitude. I learned that while cancer can be devastating, it doesn't have to change you or what's in your heart. Stay true to yourself, continue to love yourself and those around you, and you can weather anything!

—Nancy

An Inexhaustible Good Nature

An inexhaustible good nature is one of the most precious

gifts of heaven, spreading itself like oil over the troubled

sea of thought, and keeping the mind smooth

and equable in the roughest weather.

—*Washington Irving*

Wealth
Waves

Good Fortune Comes and Goes

Like everything else in life, good fortune can come and go like the tides. When we lose things that are dear to us, possessions we have worked hard for, it can be depressing. But we cannot hang onto our past predicaments.

At one point, I lost everything financially, and was about to lose my home. I spent some of the last money I had on a silent auction at a child abuse fundraiser for an artist to draw my children. At my house, he saw some of the paintings I had done, and offered to give me free art lessons. That led to an entirely new career and new passion in my life.

Material things are just things, like flotsam in the ocean. We must let them go and realize the infinite possibilities in the journey of life.

—Jane Seymour

Jane Seymour

As Boundless as the Sea

My bounty is as boundless as the sea,

My love as deep; the more I give to thee,

The more I have, for both are infinite.

—*William Shakespeare*, Romeo and Juliet

We Find Ourselves in the Sea

For whatever we lose (like a you or a me)

it's always ourselves we find in the sea.

—E. E. Cummings

In the Storm

When my husband and I were both laid off, our house went into foreclosure, and we had to file bankruptcy. I felt like I was in a storm with anxiety crashing over me and depression trying to drown me. I knew if I didn't do something positive with my life soon, I would sink deeper and deeper into the gloom. One afternoon, I was driving past the local hospital and found myself in the volunteers' office. I signed up on a whim. I now spend my time helping others. I have realized that when you think you have hit rock-bottom, there is always someone who is going through something worse. Helping other people in need takes my mind off my own problems, and it's given me a better outlook on life. I have faith in God that better times are just ahead.

—Allie

Boundless Bounty

The sea hath fish for every man.

—*William Camden*

Waiting for a Gift from the Sea

The sea does not reward those who are too anxious, too greedy, or too impatient. One should lie empty, open, choiceless as a beach—waiting for a gift from the sea.

—Anne Morrow Lindbergh

The Rabbi and the Sea

When Rabbi Akiva borrowed money from a wealthy woman, she made him promise to repay it in one month, and call on God and the sea as his guarantors. A month later, Rabbi Akiva fell ill. Desperate for her money back, the woman walked to the edge of the sea and prayed out to God. At that very moment, the daughter of Caesar, who was on a boat, took a fit of insanity and threw a chest of jewels overboard. The chest miraculously floated right to the lending woman. When Rabbi Akiva returned with his own repayment, the woman told him that his guarantors had already settled his debt. In fact, there was extra, which she donated to him.

—Traditional Jewish story

Kol man d'avid Rachmana l'tav avid.

All that God does, He does for good.

—Rabbi Akiva

Look at That Sea

Look at that sea, girls—all silver and

shadow and vision of things not seen.

We couldn't enjoy its loveliness any more

if we had millions of dollars

and ropes of diamonds.

—Lucy Maud Montgomery, Anne of Green Gables

Roll On

Roll on, thou deep and dark blue ocean, roll!

Ten thousand fleets sweep over thee in vain;

Man marks the earth with ruin—his control

Stops with the shore.

—*Lord Byron*

Let It Lift You Up

I have been through a lot over the past twelve years. My neck broke, my heart stopped, I lost jobs, I lost our home, and so much more. People ask how I can still laugh, love, smile, and joke daily. It is because I refuse to be sunk! Coming up against a big problem is a lot like coming up against a big wave. You can either do nothing and let it crash over you and drag you down, or you can kick a little and let it lift you up. When you work with the wave, it will take you places you never even dreamed possible.

—Jennifer

Cheri

Water = Life

Where the Spirit Lives

Seventy percent of the Earth's surface is covered by water. The human body is approximately sixty-five percent water. Water is where the spirit lives. Every living thing needs water to survive. And yet nearly one billion people do not have it. Some places that do have water restrict access to it for political reasons. All people have the right to clean water.

Water purifies. Water nourishes. Water is life.

We must protect our water supply, conserve it, clean it, and above all, share it.

—Jane Seymour

The Sea Is Everything

The sea is everything. It covers seven
tenths of the terrestrial globe. Its breath
is pure and healthy. It is an immense desert,
where man is never lonely,
for he feels life stirring on all sides.

—*Jules Verne, 20,000 Leagues Under the Sea*

Tied to the Ocean

It is an interesting biological fact that all of us have in our veins the exact same percentage of salt in our blood that exists in the ocean... We are tied to the ocean. And when we go back to the sea, whether it is to sail or to watch it, we are going back from whence we came.

—John F. Kennedy

Waves For Water

Jon Rose, pro-surfer-turned-humanitarian, knows about the power of the ocean and the power of being part of something bigger than himself. His charity, Waves For Water, turns other surfers and regular travelers into Clean Water Couriers by having them carry life-saving water filters in their luggage as they travel around the world.

"The idea isn't to get one person to drop off 100 filters and call it a day. Let's try to get 100,000 travelers to each pack 10 small filters, or team up with groups to implement projects with larger filters for an entire village. Then, the world will start to take notice.

Imagine millions of travelers doing this. Now, we're making waves."

—WavesForWater.org

Some Hidden Soul Beneath

There is one knows not what sweet mystery about this sea, whose gently awful stirrings seem to speak of some hidden soul beneath.

—*Herman Melville*, Moby Dick

The Ocean Would Be Less

We ourselves feel that what we are doing is just a drop in the ocean. But the ocean would be less because of that missing drop.

—Mother Teresa

Running Dry

The water crisis isn't just a global problem, it's also a local one. As I learned when I narrated the documentary, *The American Southwest: Are We Running Dry?*, for my good friend Jim Thebaut, forty percent of the residents of the Navajo Nation live without running water. Where two-thirds of the population in California lives, there are very few freshwater resources. We must stop using our most precious resource without thinking and plan for the future.

—Jane Seymour

The Power to Move Millions

Water, like religion and ideology, has the power to move millions of people. Since the very birth of human civilization, people have moved to settle close to water. People move when there is too little of it. People move when there is too much of it. People journey down it. People write and sing and dance and dream about it. People fight over it. And all people, everywhere and every day, need it... Just as we are moved by water, we must move quickly in order to save it.

—Mikhail Gorbachev

Eternal Life

But whoever drinks of the water
that I will give him will never be thirsty again.
The water that I will give him
will become in him a spring of water
welling up to eternal life.

—John 4:14

Art Titles & Descriptions

Cover: Seymour, Jane. *Remarkable Changes: The Wave III.* (triptych large)
Original acrylic on canvas, 30 x 30"

Page 2: Seymour, Jane. *Remarkable Changes: The Wave with Open Heart V.*
Mixed-media on canvas, 10 x 10"

Page 6: Seymour, Jane. *Pacific Grove II.*
Oil on canvas, 13 1/4 x 17"

Page 9: Seymour, Jane. *Symphony of Water Lilies IV.* Pastel on board, 6 x 20"

Page 10: Seymour, Jane. *Together Forever.*
Oil on canvas, 20 x 16"

Page 13: Seymour, Jane. *Open Heart Family in Teal.* Mixed-media on board, 10 x 8"

Page 14: Seymour, Jane. *Remarkable Changes: The Wave XII.* Watercolor on paper, 12 1/8 x 16 1/8"

Page 19: Seymour, Jane. *Harbor Scene.*
Watercolor on paper, 12 3/4 x 16 1/4"

Page 20: Seymour, Jane. *Remarkable Changes: The Wave I.* (small) Acrylic on canvas, 20 x 20"

Page 25: Seymour, Jane. *Pacific Grove IV.*
Oil on canvas, 14 x 18"

Page 28: Seymour, Jane. *Portrait of a Calla Lily.*
Watercolor on paper, 12 x 9"

Page 30: Seymour, Jane. *Sparkling Koi Twins IV.*
Watercolor on paper, 12 x 9"

Page 33: Photo of Jane Seymour and Tony Dovolani, from personal collection of Jane Seymour.

Page 34: Seymour, Jane. *Reflections on the Bay.*
Watercolor on paper, 6 1/8 x 9 1/8"

Page 37: Seymour, Jane. *Open Hearts Family, Mother & Child IV.* Mixed-media on board, 10 x 8"

Page 38: Ingle, Cheri. *Zen and the Art of Wave Making.* Acrylic on canvas, 20 x 15"

Page 43: Seymour, Jane. *Remarkable Changes: The Wave VIII.* Watercolor on paper, 5 x 7"

Page 44: Seymour, Jane. *Lilies in Chinese Vase with Dark Background.* Oil on canvas, 18 x 14"

Page 47: Seymour, Jane. *Peace.*
Oil on canvas, 18 x 24"

Page 50: Seymour, Jane. *Remembering Giverny.*
Oil on canvas, 24 x 30"

Page 53: Seymour, Jane. *Remarkable Changes: The Wave IX.* Watercolor on paper, 9 1/2 x 13 1/2"

Acknowledgments

Annie Gould, Sally Frankenberg, Heather Maclean,
Susan Nagy Luks, Cheri Ingle, Debra Pearl,
Susan Ginsburg, Dick Guttman, Susan Madore

Our Family: Kalen, Danya, Sierra, and Dylan; Jenni,
Chris, and Rowan; Katie, Brett, and Willa; Sean, Johnny, and Kris

Julie Trelstad, Stacy Testa, Goshia Podlaska

Our special friends at Kay Jewelers

All my dedicated, supportive fans and passionate art collectors worldwide,
who continue to inspire me by sharing their inspirational Open Hearts stories